PRAISE FOR SACRED BRAILLE

"I've read hundreds of books, articles and papers about Mary... but nothing like this. Moseley's work is not just deeply beautiful poetry that is lovely to read, it's *life-changing* poetry packed with life changing insights—life changing because you will come out of this knowing Mary and her Son better, you will be more intimate with them in a way you did not expect, and you will know yourself better in the process. All of this was a big surprise, books like this are rare, and there is no other Rosary book like this: Moseley has realized that the Rosary is divine poetry and her book taps into that amazing reality. And her book is not just poetry! The reflective questions she has toward the end truly lead to critical insights about one's relationship with God and with Our Lady. I should add I almost inevitably find questions like this lacking in some way, if not simply shallow, and that was another surprise: that these questions are not only not shallow, they are profound and so very sweetly sharp. There are many more surprises: artwork, music (yes, music!), a Marian retreat for individuals or groups, meditations on her Seven Sorrows, and on and on, all leading into Mary's Sorrowful and Immaculate Heart. As that famous song asks, 'Mary did you know?' The Catholic Church's answer to that song's question is of course a resounding *Yes*, she knew her Son is God, the Lord, the great I AM, that He would suffer out of love for us, and by diving into Moseley's poetic Rosary you will know too, and you will know it with *Mary* and through her eyes...you will come to know Mary and her Son in a new way that will astound you."

— Keith Berube, author of *Mary, the Beloved*

PRAISE FOR
SACRED BRAILLE

"*Sacred Braille* by Annabelle Moseley is vastly more than a 'how to' guide for praying the Rosary. Perfect for beginners and devotees alike, this treasury of sacred poetry, prose and art takes a most refreshing and delightfully novel approach to meditation on the sacred mysteries of the Rosary – those deep truths to which, all too often, our triple concupiscence 'blinds' us. Not unlike De Montfort's *The Secrets of the Rosary*, Moseley's book seems destined to become a classic, and is an essential addition to every public and private Catholic library."

— Jayson Brunelle,
author of *Apostles of Light of the Immaculate Heart of Mary*

"*Sacred Braille* is the vade mecum of initiation to beauty in art, religion, and prayer for the Catholic family."

— Jacques Cabaud,
author of *Is Mary Appearing Today?*

SACRED BRAILLE

The Rosary as Masterpiece
through Art, Poetry, and Reflections

ANNABELLE MOSELEY

⊕*ENROUTE*

Make the time

En Route Books and Media
5705 Rhodes Ave., St. Louis, MO 63109
Contact us at contactus@enroutebooksandmedia.com

Sacred Braille: The Rosary as Masterpiece through
Art, Poetry and Reflections

Imprimatur: ✠ Most Reverend Mark S. Rivituso,
D.D., J.C.L.
Auxiliary Bishop of St. Louis
St. Louis, MO
January 12, 2021

In accordance with CIC 827, permission to publish has been granted on January 12, 2021, by the Most Reverend Mark S. Rivituso, Auxiliary Bishop, Archdiocese of St. Louis. Permission to publish is an indication that nothing contrary to Church teaching is contained in this particular work. It does not imply any endorsement of the opinions expressed in the publication, or a general endorsement of any author; nor is any liability assumed by this permission.

Hardback ISBN: 978-1-950108-77-0
Paperback ISBN: 978-1-950108-80-0
E-book ISBN: 978-1-950108-81-7
LCCN: 2019953334

Printed in the United States of America
1 3 5 7 9 10 8 6 4 2

ACKNOWLEDGMENTS

With thanks to the venues in which some of these poems first appeared:

Dappled Things:
"Mirror Sonnet: The Annunciation"
"Mary Considers The Prophecy of Simeon"

**Adam, Eve & The Riders of the Apocalypse:
39 Contemporary Poets on the Characters of the Bible**
(Wipf and Stock, The Poiema Poetry Series, ed. D.S. Martin):

"Visitation Quartet"
"The Nativity"
"Mary Remembers Finding Jesus in the Temple"
"The Agony in the Garden"
"Mary Meets Jesus on the Way of the Cross"

With gratitude to Bishop Richard Henning for his belief in my work and his permission to photograph the art of the Seminary of the Immaculate Conception, Huntington, NY.

Interior photos of the art of the Seminary of the Immaculate Conception © 2018 Mark Staudinger. All other images of art are in the public domain. The beautiful art of the Seminary is mostly "artist unknown" and thus not attributed, the one exception being the altarpiece created by famous Jazz Age mosaic artist Hildreth Meière, which graces the Seminary crypt chapel.

Thanks to my mother, Annabelle Moseley Rufino, for her shining, faithful example, helping inspire a love of Our Lady in me from my first days.

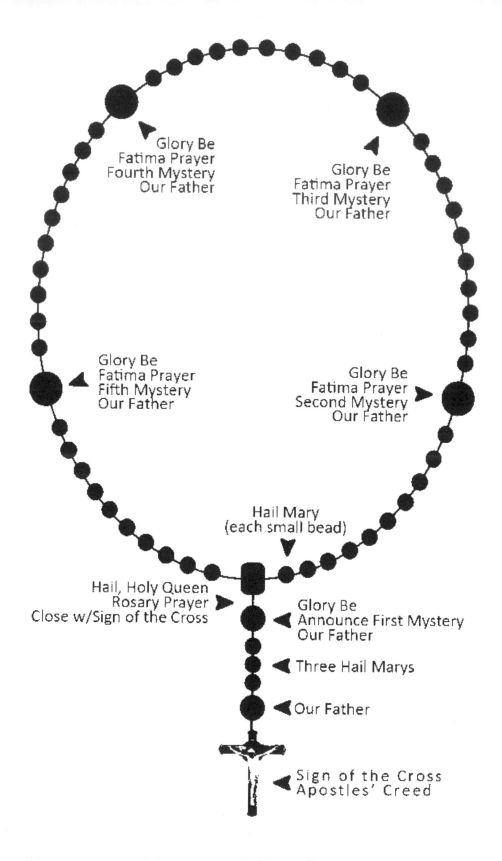

Glory Be
Fatima Prayer
Fourth Mystery
Our Father

Glory Be
Fatima Prayer
Third Mystery
Our Father

Glory Be
Fatima Prayer
Fifth Mystery
Our Father

Glory Be
Fatima Prayer
Second Mystery
Our Father

Hail Mary
(each small bead)

Hail, Holy Queen
Rosary Prayer
Close w/Sign of the Cross

Glory Be
Announce First Mystery
Our Father

Three Hail Marys

Our Father

Sign of the Cross
Apostles' Creed

CONTENTS

Reredos of the Main Chapel,
Seminary of the Immaculate Conception,
Huntington, New York

FOREWORD

Bishop Richard Henning,
Auxiliary Bishop of the Diocese of Rockville Centre

I first met Annabelle Moseley during her time as a student of theology in the Master's Program at the Seminary of the Immaculate Conception. She was an enthusiastic, hard-working, and insightful student. In particular she brought a unique perspective to the studies – the perspective of an artist immersed in beauty. In studying the Holy Scriptures, she saw the twists in the narrative, the poetry of word and imagery, and the beauty of those moments of encounter between the Lord Jesus and the cleansed or healed or forgiven.

Annabelle grasps the aesthetic theology that has always characterized Catholic faith and practice. Sadly, many contemporary Catholics know little of their rich heritage. Annabelle revels in it. She appreciates the Fathers and their creative play with biblical language. She delights in the Old and New Testament texts with their rich poetry and powerful story telling. She searches the wisdom of the devotions that have drawn countless men and women into a deeper relationship with the Lord. She opens her mind and heart to the music, sculpture, architecture, painting – all the many ways in which faith-filled artists have proclaimed truth without words.

As a poet herself, Annabelle has drawn deeply from these well springs and in this book she seeks to draw others into the mysteries. Her unique little book draws together the ancient form of the Rosary with poetry and imagery intended to reveal nuance, detail, and beauty that can only come through the grace of contemplation. She searches the "DNA" of prayer and the life of faith, inviting the reader into a double helix of Rosary and *Lectio Divina*. Sacred art, Sacred Word and Sacred Braille surround the visitor to the pages of this book – a book that asks more than passive reading. It challenges us to contemplation and participation in the mystery of Divine Love.

This book was especially meaningful to me because it incorporates imagery from the Seminary of the Immaculate Conception – a place that I called home for many happy years. In particular, Annabelle includes carved and gilded panels from the great *reredos* that serves as the central focus of the beautiful Byzantine Romanesque chapel. I believe that this great hand-carved work partly inspired Annabelle's insights regarding the interplay of beauty, word, and faith. Standing behind the altar, the anonymous work offers a summary of the story and truth of salvation. At its center, there is a large crucifixion scene – the ugliest of moments offered as a thing of intense beauty. It depicts death while leading the believer to the truth that this death is life for the world. At the "dome of the heavens" high above the scene are words taken from the Gospel of John, "when I am lifted up all nations will be drawn to me." In this the work proclaims the universal saving significance of this moment for all people and for all creation. In the scene itself, the image of the crucified Christ is set into an abstract representation of the holy womb that bore Him into the world. The gifts of the Spirit flow from that womb of new life. At the foot of the cross, the truth of death become life is expressed in the Medieval image of the pelican mother piercing her own breast and saving her hungry chicks with her own life's blood. Around the central panel the work incorporates small carved panels depicting scenes from the Gospel. In those scenes of healing, mercy, and redemption the viewer is drawn into the totality of the Gospel story. The images are meant to be read against the central panel of the cross – for it is there that you see the truth of the death that is displayed – the truth that it is the supreme act of love and a moment of re-creation and new life. And the cross in the central scene deepens the understanding of the compassion and power on display in the many panels – these are more than images of a wonder worker or great preacher – this is the work of the Living God – the work of healing, reconciling, and restoring creation. But it is precisely in its place in the daily celebration of the Mass that this work finds its context and deepest power. For there it reflects the glory of the True Cross and Love itself. This great carved work, like Annabelle's tactile language of Sacred Braille, opens the eyes of the heart to the wonder of God's Self Gift.

I hope that you will do more than read this book. I hope that you will immerse yourself in the mysteries that it evokes. I hope that you will return again and again to contemplate and reflect, to pray and to listen. I hope that as it draws you closer to the Lord, it will also bring you to deeper communion with other men and women of faith. Its exercises are meant to do just that – to allow that mutual gift of question and witness to plunge us into the depths.

We all owe a debt of gratitude for the gifts that the Lord has bestowed upon Annabelle and for the quality of her enthusiastic response and use of those gifts for our sake. May her witness, and this book, be a gift that brings us to new insight and deeper faith.

Sandro Botticelli
"The Virgin and Child (Madonna of the Book)"

PREFACE

I. Sacred Braille:
Encountering the Rosary as Tangible Language

"In the beginning was the Word, and the Word was with God, and the Word was God. He was with God in the beginning. Through Him all things were made, and without Him nothing was made that has been made. In him was life, and that life was the light of all mankind. The light shines in the darkness, and the darkness has not overcome it. There was a man sent from God whose name was John. He came as a witness to testify concerning that light, so that through him all might believe. He himself was not the light; he came only as a witness to the light. The true light that gives light to everyone was coming into the world. He was in the world, and though the world was made through him, the world did not recognize him. He came to that which was his own, but his own did not receive him. Yet to all who did receive him, to those who believed in his name, he gave the right to become children of God—children born not of natural descent, nor of human decision or a husband's will, but born of God. The Word became flesh and made his dwelling among us. We have seen his glory, the glory of the one and only Son, who came from the Father, full of grace and truth. John testified concerning him. He cried out, saying, "This is the one I spoke about when I said, 'He who comes after me has surpassed me because he was before me.'"" (Jn 1:1-15)

Language is the way human beings form thoughts and feelings into words. We listen to words, speak words, read and write them. Good writing is like an extended and elevated form of talking and good reading is like an extended and elevated form of listening. Braille, as we know, is a tactile language for the blind, in which characters are represented by raised dots that can be felt with the hands. Are we not all, to some extent, blind? "He was in the world, and though the world was made through him, the world did not recognize him" (Jn 1:10). Even those of us who love him, sin; and we can be blind to the very presence of Christ in our daily lives. The Rosary, when prayed regularly, can help us to recognize Him. Through the gift of its Braille formed by simple beads, it cultivates the interior vision we need to see with more clarity.

What better gift could Our Lady have given us than the Rosary? The Rosary is Sacred Braille, in that it is an amazing juxtaposition of a language of prayer we can feel with our hands, joining word to touch. It is the Rosary to which our fingers may cling, as our flesh craves something tangible. The decades of the Rosary can be thought about, and, quite literally, felt, at the same time. While contemporary society separates the ideas of "thinking" and "feeling," Scripture unites all functions in the heart. If we meditate on the words, "Mary treasured up all these things and pondered them in her heart," (Lk 2:19) the thinking and feeling functions are joined. The Rosary, through engaging both thought and touch, unites our spiritual and physical natures; our thinking and feeling (both in the sense of touch and emotion) faculties.

We need no sight to pray the Rosary, yet it cultivates our spiritual vision. Cling to the beads of the Rosary in the middle of a frightened night and you will experience the light of tangible language, of tactile prayer, of Sacred Braille. The title of this book, *Sacred Braille*, reminds that the beads our fingers travel make up a tactile pilgrimage of prayer. (The Rosary provides a pilgrimage we take with our fingers.) The Rosary is a tangible masterpiece. As surely as one who is blind can read Shakespeare and the Psalms through books of Braille, their fingers journeying the raised textures in a felt language, one who needs the light of greater faith can grip the beads of their Rosary even in a dark night, and feel their way through a circular journey, deeper into closeness with God and His Mother. It's a journey we take without need for any vision but an interior one; without the need for any locomotion except the touch of a hand. Simply put, it's a pilgrimage to our true home.

Titian
"The Presentation of the Virgin Mary"

II. Holding Hands with Mystery and Masterpiece

What if you don't have Rosary beads to hold while praying? Your fingers form a decade, a Braille of flesh and blood. Touch each of your own fingers as you would one of the Rosary's beads, and ask that Mary and the Fruit of her Womb bless your hands and help them to do God's work.

With that in mind, let's roll up our sleeves and start by looking at the components of the Rosary. There are Our Fathers (Known as The Lord's Prayer) there are Hail Marys and there are Glory Be's. Those are the three best-known prayers to Catholics. There is also a Preparatory Prayer and The Apostles Creed that should ideally be prayed before the Rosary and a prayer called "O My Jesus" after each decade, and the "Hail Holy Queen" at the end of the Rosary. There are other recommended prayers, too, that can be added, although their inclusion is not necessary.

Please don't let the worry that you are not praying the Rosary "perfectly" keep you from trying. Any amount of prayer in the Rosary is worthwhile, if done with a loving heart. This book will give you all you need to pray a complete Rosary (for a full guide on the components of the Rosary, see page 123), but for now, let's just talk about all those Hail Marys.

Let's begin with the first three, that beautiful little trinity of beads all by itself after the crucifix and before the first decade. For starters, it's wonderful to remember that we are asked to pray for a different grace with each of those beads: first Faith, then Hope, then Love.

So to begin, as you pray the first three Hail Marys, meditate on each virtue and ask to receive them as blessings in your life, or in the life of the person for whom you are praying.

What about all the other Hail Marys? There are 10 in each decade. Have you ever heard the following criticism of the Rosary? "It's just so repetitive. I start to feel like I am just parroting after a while." The Rosary is not meant to be easy. Something that can be richly rewarding, yes. But easy? No. It is a spiritual discipline; it's exercise. Exercise feels so much more better once a routine is established. Same with the Rosary. Countless saints assure us Mary takes great delight and comfort in our Rosary and that it can do great good for our individual lives and for the healing of the whole world.

Still, how will you answer such criticism as "too long to pray" or "repetitive" when it wells up from someone you know; or even from yourself? St. Francis was asked by Jesus, "Give me something," to which Francis replied, "I have nothing left to give. I have already given you all of my love." Jesus answered, "Francis, give me it all again and again. It will give me the same pleasure."

In a similar way, each of the Hail Marys is a way of saying "I love you." You are repeating her treasured greeting from the angel Gabriel and giving her the gift of the words she most loves to hear.

Think about this: Can you ever really tire of telling your beloved, "I love you?" It will never be enough. Just because you told them a few hours ago does not cheapen the renewal of love; it is still music to the ears.

Here is a deeply personal story I will share with you. When my father was dying, I asked to ride in the ambulance at his side. I was eleven years old. When I say I asked, I really mean I insisted, stubbornly. I knew, somehow, it was very important that I be there. My mother and I got in the ambulance, never leaving my father's side, and each of us took one of his hands. My father was still holding on to consciousness, though he could not speak. I remember studying his hands so I could memorize the feel of them, the palm and fingers. And in the last litany I spoke to him, I repeated the words "I love you," again and again as the screaming ambulance sped its way to the hospital. It was the only thing I wanted to say. In that space, it was all that mattered. I kissed his hand, pressed it to my cheek, held it strongly in my two little hands. It never occurred to me that I was being repetitive or that one "I love you" was enough. I wanted to fill a lifetime of "I love you"s into his being while I knew he could still hear me.

This, I believe, is how one ought to approach the Rosary. It is a chance to hold Mary's hands, and to also hold the hands of Christ. There are ten beads per decade just as there are ten fingers on a hand. The criticism one often hears about the Rosary: "It's so repetitive," fades when one thinks of each "Hail Mary" as an "I love you." Can "I love you" ever be said too much to a beloved spouse, a dear child, an honored parent? No. There is no such thing as too much when it comes to those words, and the emotion behind them.

The next time you find yourself finding the Rosary "repetitive," "too long," or even "boring," see it as a way to clasp Mary's two hands in yours. Each bead in a decade becomes one of her beautiful fingers… fingers that cared for Jesus when he was a child, fingers that touched him as he died. Each bead in a decade becomes a way to clasp the hands of Jesus into your own... the hands so extremely pained with their wounds of love. Each bead in a decade is a way to thank him, to touch his strong and sacrificing fingers as his little one who loves him and never tires of telling him so. The "Hail Marys" and "Our Fathers" are divine "I love you"s.

If you are reading this, it just might be that you are meant to encounter a greater devotion to the Rosary. We must acknowledge a simple fact. Some among us already love the Rosary. You know who you are. Some among us find the practice of the Rosary challenging. You know who you are. My answer to both types of people reading this book is that it has been designed with you in mind. Whether you pray the Rosary daily, or whether you occasionally or rarely do... even if you never have. This book, written with prayer, has been designed hoping to bring new ardor to your experience of the Rosary.

I finished this book on September 8, 2019 on the Feast of the Nativity of the Blessed Virgin Mary. It was prepared for publication during October, the month of the Holy Rosary and published on November 21, 2019, on the Feast of the Presentation of the Blessed Virgin Mary in the Temple, celebrating the day on which Mary was brought by her parents Sts. Joachim and Anna to the Temple in Jerusalem and consecrated to God. It is a fitting day to bring this book out into the world, as the reader is invited to follow Mary's example and make the choice to fully surrender his or her life to God. The poems in this book were written to transport the reader into the midst of each mystery of the Rosary. The art chosen is meant to do the same. After all, the Rosary is a Masterpiece of prayer, at home with works of art. This book also contains a compendium of prayers, reflections and a Bonus

3-Day Retreat I designed for those in private or group settings. As a way to pay further homage to Our Lady, I included art, poetry, and meditations on the Seven Sorrows Devotion. Thank you for reading Sacred Braille. Come on in; and welcome. May God bless you on your pilgrimage, dear reader.

For when you pray the Rosary, you're embarking on what I call the "Pilgrimage of The Crowns": the Crown of Mary, the Crown of Christ, and the Crown of Roses (Rosary) that joins us to Jesus and Mary. Through Grace, the Crown of Roses will help us on our quest to receive what God has ready for those who love Him. "Be you faithful unto death, and I will give you a crown of life."(Rev 2:10)

May your life give homage to the crowns, and may you hold hands with the mysteries.

—Annabelle Moseley
Ad majórem Dei glóriam

Leopold Kupelwieser
"Immaculate Heart of Mary"

Giovanni Battista Paggi
"Madonna of the Rosary"

DEDICATION

When I was six years old, my grandfather told me, "If you ever need anything, ask Mary. Turn to Our Lady in prayer." One morning, when I was seven years old, I awakened to see, beside my pillow, an antique-style pin with a portrait of Our Lady on it. My family members were taken aback when I asked who had left me such a lovely gift. To this day, they attest they had never seen it before. Even at my tender age, I saw this as a miraculous gift of love. This pin, along with my grandfather's words, helped me get through tragic loss in childhood. I believe Our Lady, in her compassion, reached out to me, knowing what would come, so that I would have her to comfort and strengthen me. I dedicate this book...

TO OUR LADY OF THE ROSARY
Hoc placet accipere paolo donum

Albrecht Dürer
"The Seven Sorrows of the Virgin"

THE SEVEN
SORROWS OF MARY

Annabelle Moseley

THE FIRST SORROW

MIRROR SONNET*:
MARY RECALLS THE PROPHECY OF SIMEON

A mother knows her son's hands like her own.
She studies them from birth—each fingernail
is halo-shaped. Soft skin over strong bone,
each line and dimple forms a Sacred Braille.
While Simeon foretold, I held Christ's hand.
And that was when the blade first pierced my soul.
I knew that to redeem a broken land,
my child's palms could not remain smooth, whole.
The earth is punctured, seeded, before sprouts
grow forth. Then fruit is gathered, branches pruned.
There must be something for the soul who doubts
to press their fingers into, like a wound.
The piercing of my soul provides a sieve—
for sifting death from those who long to live.

For sifting death from those who long to live,
the piercing of my soul provides a sieve—
to press their fingers into, like a wound.
There must be something for the soul who doubts.
Grow forth! Then fruit is gathered, branches pruned.
The earth is punctured, seeded, before sprouts.
My child's palms could not remain smooth, whole.
I knew that—to redeem a broken land...
And that was when the blade first pierced my soul.
While Simeon foretold, I held Christ's hand.
Each line and dimple formed a Sacred Braille,
was halo-shaped. Soft skin over strong bone,
I'd studied them from birth—each fingernail.
A mother knows her son's hands like her own.

* a new poetic form created by the author

Annabelle Moseley

THE SECOND SORROW

MARY REMEMBERS THE FLIGHT INTO EGYPT

The smell of myrrh, like death, clings to my hair,
while Joseph scans each tree for Herod's spies—
and anguish is the incense of our prayer.
Our bag is packed with tribute from The Wise,
but I've forgotten all that gleams within—
although that gold will lighten our escape.
Keeping my child close against my skin,
my arms defend his warm and rounded shape.
For on this night of kings, Bethlehem bleeds.
The stars above me stare like children's eyes,
a constellation shaped in grievous deeds.
The three men found my son by those same skies.
And my epiphany is that this flight
begins one lifelong sacrificial night.

Annabelle Moseley

The Third Sorrow

Paolo Veronese
"Christ Among the Doctors" (detail)

MARY RECALLS THE LOSS
OF THE CHILD IN THE TEMPLE

For three long days we looked. Our son was gone.
The "yes" that I had given for his life—
my "let it be done unto me," like dawn,
had grown into mid-morning: bold. The knife
piercing me, sharp as midnight? I had lost
my light, my son, my God—my own dear flesh.
I'd always known such love would bear great cost.
He was a growing boy, no static creche—
I could not keep him always at my side.
My sorrow peaked like Egypt's pyramids.
He'd come to reconcile and divide.
I feared the ones he'd die for would make bids
upon his life. So as we searched for him,
a canticle of sunset was my hymn.

Annabelle Moseley

THE FOURTH SORROW

Mary Meets Jesus on the Way of the Cross

When he was not yet two, he hurt himself.
He found his father's bench, climbed up the rail,
and reaching for a hammer on the shelf,
he pricked his finger on a sharpened nail—
and cried out. Holding him, I was dismayed
to see five beads of blood fall to the ground.
Between torment and love, my spirit swayed.
Each drop looked like a red rose petal—round
and bright. This, just a small wound, still I longed
to gather every floret of his pain
because it was a part of him, belonged
inside the reliquary of his veins,
or washed by God-sent rain or shared, adored.
In each drop was an endless vineyard stored.

In each drop was an endless vineyard stored.
And as he staggered toward me with the cross,
seeing his gaping wounds, the blood that poured,
hearing the women wailing for my loss,
my heart quickened and opened like a rose
in torment and in love, to take each thorn
they crowned him with into myself—enclose
each trace of lost blood, pain. Since he was born,
I knew this day would come. I didn't know
that as our eyes met, I would see the child
that he had been, those many years ago.
I tell you, as he caught my eyes, he smiled—
through pain, to comfort me. His march resumed—
and each red drop he shed anointed, bloomed.

Annabelle Moseley

THE FIFTH SORROW

MARY RECALLS THE CRUCIFIXION

When Abraham led Isaac to the knife
an angel stopped his fearful act of love.
Here I present to God my child's life—
as after he was born. Each turtle dove
my husband and I offered, while I held
our infant closely, signified release.
His consecrated will would be upheld.
I will not seek to gain Abraham's peace
today. I know my child will be killed—
in willing adoration. I stay near,
and stroke his feet. His swollen eyes are filled
with blood. You ask me what I feel? Not fear,
but sorrow's insect tearing me with stings—
new labor pains, a pull like rushing wings.

New labor pains, a pull like rushing wings,
my breathing quickens as his muscles twitch.
Abraham's vast descendants: slaves and kings—
How many million more souls can Christ stitch
into his cradle crown with every thorn?
How many children Calvary will birth.
His arms are spread wide, like when he was born—
as though he measured, east to west, the worth
of all the world and found it very good.
He didn't cry. I loved his perfect mouth.
I still do, as he sighs upon the wood—
the sacred compass rooting north to south.
I love this child more than my own breath.
With one last cry, *his* labor conquers death.

Annabelle Moseley

THE SIXTH SORROW

William Adolphe Bouguereau
"Pieta"

MIRROR SONNET:
MARY PREPARES THE BODY OF JESUS FOR BURIAL

After my son was born, I swaddled him—
wrapping with linen cloth to keep him warm,
securely binding every outstretched limb.
His body now takes such a different form.
He is so still. Sometimes I'd guard his sleep
in childhood, my vigil—feel him breathe.
Tonight, we swathe his death. The watch we keep:
cleaning his wounds, anointing, helping sheathe
the sword of peace who conquered death and sin.
We treat his scars with myrrh, bandage his sores,
pray for the floods of sorrow to begin
transforming, wine-like, into hope-filled stores.
For now, torment has filled my very soul—
torn like the temple curtain, and yet whole.

Torn like the temple curtain, and yet whole,
for now, torment has filled my very soul.
Transforming, wine-like, into hope-filled stores—
pray for the floods of sorrow to begin.
We treat his scars with myrrh, bandage his sores—
the sword of peace who conquered death and sin.
Cleaning his wounds, anointing, helping sheathe,
tonight, we swathe his death. This watch we keep.
In childhood, my vigil felt him breathe.
He is so still. Sometimes I'd guard his sleep.
His body now takes such a different form.
Securely binding every outstretched limb,
wrapping with linen cloth to keep him warm.
After my son was born, I swaddled him.

THE SEVENTH SORROW

Caravaggio
"The Deposition"

MIRROR SONNET:
MARY DESCRIBES THE BURIAL OF JESUS

A grave within a garden, garden grave.
Tonight among the trees and ancient stone,
we planted he who faced the scythe to save,
we gave the root of Jesse, blood and bone.
Within a rock-hewn tomb, we placed the vine.
Though he was cut, he still bore every branch.
A place of rot and growth holds Jesus' shrine.
Here Eden's tears and blood, his grave will stanch—
for my son nourishes the earth's deep thirst.
Gethsemane received his blood as rain.
I long to follow him, the boy I nursed,
inside the cave to pacify my pain.
But that thought passes. Recollect his light.
I wonder where his soul's seed rests tonight.

I wonder where his soul's seed rests tonight.
But that thought passes. Recollect his light.
Inside the cave, to pacify my pain,
I want to follow him, the boy I nursed.
Gethsemane received his blood as rain,
for my son nourishes the earth's deep thirst—
here Eden's tears and blood, his grave will stanch.
This place of rot and growth holds Jesus' shrine.
Though he was cut, he still bore every branch.
Within a rock-hewn tomb, we placed the vine.
We gave the root of Jesse, blood and bone.
We planted he who faced the scythe to save,
Among the vibrant blooms and ancient stone—
a grave within a garden, garden grave.

Raphael
"Madonna of Loreto"

THE JOYFUL MYSTERIES

Annabelle Moseley

THE FIRST JOYFUL MYSTERY
Fruit of the Mystery: Humility

MIRROR SONNET:
MARY REMEMBERS THE ANNUNCIATION

In spring, Israel's almond trees are clouds
of petals, wrapping bark in pink and white.
The blossom branches, like bride's veils, or shrouds—
eager to hold God's embryonic light.
It was just after dawn. I'd walked outside
with sacred longing's wildflower prayer.
The angel's words engulfed me like a tide.
I swam into the blessing and the dare.
There in the courtyard, crimson poppies bloomed
among the grass, like rubies, or like blood.
There when I breathed the almond air, perfumed,
my womb was spring, God's Word a new-formed bud.
In prayer, I knelt to gather blooms of red—
my joyful sacrifice, the yes I'd said.

My joyful sacrifice: the yes I'd said.
In prayer, I knelt to gather blooms of red—
my womb was spring, God's Word a new-formed bud,
there when I breathed the almond air, perfumed.
Among the grass, like rubies, or like blood,
there in the courtyard, crimson poppies bloomed.
I swam into the blessing and the dare.
The angel's words engulfed me like a tide,
with sacred longing's wildflower prayer.
It was just after dawn. I'd walked outside
eager to hold God's embryonic light.
The blossom branches, like bride's veils, or shrouds
of petals, wrapping bark in pink and white.
In spring, Israel's almond trees are clouds.

Annabelle Moseley

THE SECOND JOYFUL MYSTERY
Fruit of the Mystery: Love of Neighbor

Mariotto Albertinelli
"Visitation"

VISITATION QUARTET

In one embrace: Elizabeth and John—
Jesus and Mary. As the women met,
two pregnancies entwined. Their men looked on.
God's instruments bowed, in a string quartet.
Their wombs, like violins, held pulsing song.
The Baptist leapt in joy—the Savior trilled.
And cello-like, Elizabeth's voice, strong,
gave blessing for belief that was fulfilled.
As a viola, Mary's psalm sustained.
Her harmony, a humble inner voice,
enraptured as it echoed. Wild—trained
in grace, gave their unborn call to rejoice.
It was both canticle and battle cry,
Sonata of surrender—lullaby.

THE THIRD JOYFUL MYSTERY
Fruit of the Mystery:
Poverty of Spirit, Detachment from
the Things of the World

MATT. 2.2

THE NATIVITY

"She gave birth," Scripture says. One line to tell
of Mary's sacrifice. A mother knows
how much that means—the way each tiny cell
within each muscle feels a labor's throes.
And yet a mother wills the searing pain.
Her suffering allows her dear one birth.
And through a mother's long, heroic strain,
she focuses upon the gift's great worth.
Mary's libation, offered up to God
presented love through body, soul, and will.
She felt him near, she almost felt him nod.
For through Christ's passion, God's Word would fulfill—
through water and through blood, deliver all
to life—pushing through Calvary's grim caul.

THE FOURTH JOYFUL MYSTERY
Fruit of the Mystery: Obedience

MARY RECALLS THE PRESENTATION

When Simeon approached, his widened eyes
and trembling hands foretold his prophecy.
And as he spoke, in words solemn and wise,
we learned about the path he could foresee.
A parent often thinks about the way
their child will grow up to change the world.
Joseph and I had blessed the shining day
that we presented Jesus—sleeping, curled
cob tight within our arms. As that man spoke,
I knew this day was his as much as ours.
As our amazement rose, his hope awoke—
prepared him for his death, due in mere hours.
He kissed my hand and then he bowed, withdrew.
That night I dreamed a curtain tore in two.

Annabelle Moseley

THE FIFTH JOYFUL MYSTERY
Fruit of the Mystery:
Piety, Greater Devotion to Jesus

LUC. II. 67

MARY REMEMBERS FINDING JESUS IN THE TEMPLE

What joy it was to see his face again,
to feel his arms around me as I clung.
His eyes were like a merciful Amen,
reflecting how mere days without him stung.
The storm was over now. Our fears were stilled.
Jesus invited us to walk across
the ocean of acceptance that he willed.
For someday he would die upon the cross,
and did not want for us to wonder where
his soul had gone. This test had been our sign.
His loved ones could mourn, weep—but not despair.
He was not gone, but held by the divine—
about his Father's business for three days.
Trust. Even in a loss, God must be praised.

Fra Angelico
"Lamentation over Christ" (1440-1442)

THE SORROWFUL MYSTERIES

Annabelle Moseley

THE FIRST SORROWFUL MYSTERY
Fruit of the Mystery:
Contrition, Conformity to the Will of God, Trust in God

Fra Angelico
"Agony in the Garden"

THE AGONY IN THE GARDEN

Within a garden like this we were lost.
Eden was rooted to Gethsemane—
We slept while you kept watch and mourned the cost—
gazing at moonlight through the olive trees.
Your red drops fell, consoling Abel's blood
which once cried out from deep within the earth.
Your tears and sweat baptized and blessed the mud.
Sacrificed slumber would have had great worth.
You'd barred us from nightmares: forbidden fruit
we tasted in our dreams. You gave true bread.
We could have nourished you, provided shoots
of strength for branch-deep weariness. Instead,
we closed our eyes, with everything at stake.
All we'd been asked to do was stay awake.

Annabelle Moseley

THE SECOND SORROWFUL MYSTERY
Fruit of the Mystery: Purity, Mortification

THE SCOURGING OF JESUS AT THE PILLAR

The Rosary's second sorrow-mystery
is touched by human flesh on polished beads.
Our fingers press the rounded history
of how the rose was cut to spare the weeds.
Some want to look away, some want to run.
Even in prayer, this image is a bruise
that chafes the eyes—to see God's only son
betrayed and bound for sinners to abuse.
But as we hold this decade's beads, seed-small,
We feel Christ's trembling hand amid the pain.
The whisper of our prayer becomes a call
to him, transcending time—like light through rain.
Let us not run. Let us not look away.
In solidarity of love, we stay.

THE THIRD SORROWFUL MYSTERY
Fruit of the Mystery: Fortitude, Moral Courage

MIRROR SONNET:
JESUS IS CROWNED WITH THORNS

They didn't know that they had crowned a king
who, oyster-like, could turn grit into pearl,
transform a thorn crown to a royal ring—
garlands of life made from a twisted swirl.
They did not understand that he could shape
healing from hatred, blessing from a curse.
Clothed in his sacrifice, he wore the cape
they draped on him to mock, to wound him worse—
a blood-red cloak of pain; a rose in rain.
Seventy thorns entered his vine-draped head,
trespassed the veins of thought branching his brain.
Matting his hair, new buds sprung, where he bled.
Each thorn, upon its entrance, recognized
the mind of its creator, paradise.

The mind of its creator: paradise—
each thorn, upon its entrance, recognized.
Matting his hair, new buds sprung, where he bled,
trespassed the veins of thought branching his brain.
Seventy thorns entered his vine-draped head.
A blood-red cloak of pain—(a rose in rain)
they draped on him to mock, to wound him worse.
Clothed in his sacrifice, he wore the cape:
healing from hatred, blessing from a curse.
They did not understand that he could shape
garlands of life made from a twisted swirl,
transform a thorn crown to a royal ring
that, oyster-like, could turn grit into pearl.
They didn't know that they had crowned a king.

Annabelle Moseley

THE FOURTH SORROWFUL MYSTERY
Fruit of the Mystery:
Patience, Perseverance in Trials

Titian
"Christ Carrying the Cross"

SIMON RECALLS THE CARRYING OF THE CROSS

This is my canticle—I bless the beam
that pressed into my shoulder in his stead.
It happened like something out of a dream.
The weight of that could kill him, I had said
under my breath. Somehow the soldiers heard—
commanded me to take it in his place.
I felt the mass of earth and stars conferred
upon my back, yet knew it was a grace—
because his blood had smeared upon the wood
and it was that which gave me strength to walk.
To bear his cross is pain, a burdened good.
Given the chance, accept it. Do not balk.
Simon means "he who hears and then obeys"—
That's all. I'm anyone who trusts and prays.

THE FIFTH SORROWFUL MYSTERY

Fruit of the Mystery:
Salvation, Self-Denial, Forgiveness of Others

THE CRUCIFIXION,
THROUGH THE EYES OF THE GOOD THIEF

It was the only good thing I had known
in all my life—to die beside my God.
Before now, hate was all that I'd been shown.
I was a sinner, stealer and a fraud.
My arms were forced apart, splayed out in fear.
His arms opened in love—willing embrace.
I wished that I could bend and bow, revere
his feet, then wipe the blood from his good face.
Instead I called across the space between
his cross and mine—and that was oceans wide.
For he was innocence. His heart was clean
and knew how I had hated, envied, lied.
And yet he promised me today. Today.
The world had told me, *Leave*. God told me, *Stay*.

Hildreth Meière
"Christ Pantocrator" (detail)

THE GLORIOUS
MYSTERIES

Annabelle Moseley

THE FIRST GLORIOUS MYSTERY
Fruit of the Mystery: Faith

MARY MAGDALENE DESCRIBES THE RESURRECTION

Disconsolate, my weeping blinded me
to angels lounging in his tomb, the gift
they claimed—to sit where he had lain—must be
a warmth that pierces stone. And yet the rift
within my heart could only feel his loss.
Their vigil hailed new life. Mine was a cry
that longed to cling, a garden-shroud of moss.
What made me turn around? I wondered why
the angels' eyes had filled with tears of light.
Correctly—I beheld a gardener.
He spoke my name, fully restored my sight
to see all that had bloomed. "Good Pardoner,
you've made it spring, flowered forth from the grave—
an herb of lasting sweetness from the cave."

An herb of lasting sweetness from the cave,
I tried to cling to him—instead, received
a sacred mission: "Spread my word." He gave
this task to send my heart, so deeply grieved,
in service to bind up my wounds and theirs.
His words were tendrils climbing as he'd speak—
a vine to strengthen and console his heirs.
"Why are you crying? Who is it you seek?"
Each word's petal was bold, and had a smell
like frankincense and honey. This bouquet,
I'd bring to the apostles. I would tell
his mourning ones: I spoke with him today.
In death, I sought my Lord. But what I found?
My Lord God Gardener, raised from the ground.

Annabelle Moseley

THE SECOND GLORIOUS MYSTERY
Fruit of the Mystery: Hope, Desire for Heaven

THE APOSTLES RECALL THE ASCENSION

One last embrace, one last shared meal of fish—
we miss you from the moment that you rise.
Though you've not left us orphans, still we wish
that we could cling as you ascend the skies.
Who can explain the way we need your hand—
how your resonant voice comforts our ears?
No one on earth can know us, understand
the way you do. We want more time—more years.
The clouds around you are unleavened bread.
The sky above—Annunciation-blue.
We stand there until sunset, orange-red
and purple, jewel the firmament. Our view
of heaven's jubilation folds to black
on our walk home, lonely—wanting you back.

The Third Glorious Mystery
Fruit of the Mystery: Gifts of the Holy Spirit, Wisdom, Love of God

Jean Restout II
"Pentecost" (detail)

PETER DESCRIBES THE
COMING OF THE HOLY SPIRIT

He had named me his rock and sought to build
upon my back. I felt more chalk than stone.
And then the bellowing came—house was filled
with wind. I felt him calling in the bone
and marrow of me. Blood-deep, filled with storm,
a zeal-strong wind would be what it would take
to strengthen weak denial, change my form
to rugged. Everything was now at stake.
The fire brought language, words forged in flame.
I tasted singed vowels, yet felt no pain,
only the burn of wanting speech to claim
as many souls as I could tell, explain
the parable of a man made of chalk,
God's wind and fire transformed into rock.

Annabelle Moseley

THE FOURTH GLORIOUS MYSTERY
Fruit of the Mystery: Devotion to Mary

Titian
"Assumption of the Virgin"

JOHN SPEAKS TO MARY BEFORE THE ASSUMPTION

The veins within your hands are lines I read
as scripture. And your eyes that saw him dead
and also saw him born, see what we need
and are unbearable beauty: stars spread
with layered mercy trembling in your gaze.
Your shoulders, strong, beneath your hair and veil.
I sing your beauty, grace-filled, countless ways.
You are near death. I kneel before you, hail
my mother. Here your child sings the womb
that held the Word made flesh, that taught him speech.
Your voice and face consoled him till the tomb.
Be near to me forever, I beseech.
While your body is still this side of sky,
I hold your hand, so hard to say goodbye.

For blessed is the fruit of your womb, who,
while he hung outstretched, dying on the cross
gave me to be your son and gave me you
to be my mother— gain amidst the loss.
And you, the tabernacle of his life
became the eyes through which I could see him.
He looked so much like you. You ease the strife
of all who you encounter. You're the hymn
of love enfleshed—and strong, a river reed—
who faced the wind while teaching how to bow.
You and your son are all I'll ever need.
My heart's a field. His teachings are the plow.
Then let me be made little as a seed
and hold me in your palm. That's all I need.

Annabelle Moseley

THE FIFTH GLORIOUS MYSTERY
Fruit of the Mystery: Final Perseverance, Eternal Happiness

Fra Angelico
"Coronation of the Virgin"

MIRROR SONNET: MARY, AS SHE IS CROWNED

A mother knows her son's hands like her own.
As he holds up a starry diadem,
I'm looking at his transformed flesh and bone—
Recalling newborn hands in Bethlehem,
the myrrh I smoothed into his wounded palms.
And now I see the sky through them: pure light.
Those chasms are more beautiful than psalms.
His marked hands are my sorrow and delight.
A gleaming crescent moon supports my feet.
The sun, stripped of its burn, wraps me in glow
A throne of pearl is given as my seat.
I'm back with him again—that's all I know.
I clasp his hand. Each finger is my jewel.
I'd do it all again. That is my rule.

I'd do it all again. That is my rule.
I clasp his hand. Each finger is my jewel.
I'm back with him again—that's all I know.
A throne of pearl is given as my seat.
The sun, stripped of its burn, wraps me in glow
A gleaming crescent moon supports my feet.
His marked hands are my sorrow and delight;
Those chasms are more beautiful than psalms.
Through them, I see the sky. Through them, pure light—
I once smoothed myrrh into those wounded palms.
Recalling newborn hands in Bethlehem,
I'm looking at his transformed flesh and bone—
as he holds up a starry diadem.
A mother knows her son's hands like her own.

The Luminous
Mysteries

THE FIRST LUMINOUS MYSTERY
Fruit of the Mystery:
Openness to the Holy Spirit

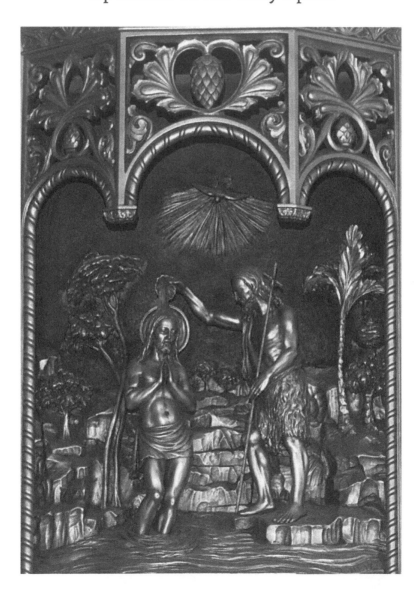

THE BAPTISM OF JESUS IN THE RIVER JORDAN

The Jordan River was a font of light,
reflecting green trees crowned with swaying leaves.
The Baptist's eyes shone passionately bright—
his arms outstretched to soldiers as to thieves.
No one who sought baptism was denied.
The rugged man who dressed in camel skins
shared wild honey—faith, offered to guide
repentance under waves, new life begins.
When Jesus came, and bowed his head, then bid
John to submerge God in the river's tomb—
the two embraced the way their mothers did
when they themselves were still within the womb.
Like two halves of a scallop shell, they met,
forming a pearl of strength against death's threat.

Annabelle Moseley

The Second Luminous Mystery
Fruit of the Mystery: Mary's Intercession

Giorgio Vasari
"Marriage at Cana"

TO JESUS, AT THE WEDDING FEAST AT CANA

Like wine, your days of freedom have run short.
The lyre and the flute play sweetly still—
the wedding dancers carelessly cavort,
but you have come to do your mother's will.
You take six jars and fill them to the brim.
And as the water flows you say goodbye
to your life as a private person, dim
the light on who you were, prepare to die.
A carpenter knows when the wood is planed
enough. You might have liked more time to smooth
your readiness for what had been ordained.
Instead you gave your splintered joy and youth.
This is your wedding too. Tonight you give
yourself to ministry; that we might live.

Annabelle Moseley

The Third Luminous Mystery
Fruit of the Mystery:
Repentance, Christian Witness &
Conversion, Trust in God

THE KINGDOM OF GOD

The one who in the wilderness cried out
has decreased, like a waning summer moon.
Be reconciled, quickly. Do not doubt.
The time is not someday—not even soon.
It's close as palm and fingers, knuckles, wrist.
Your folded hands in prayer are two stopped clocks.
Enter His gate. Do more than just subsist.
Like sunrise, His light lifts the ripe corn stalks,
saving the ones who gaze upon His face.
The wind and rain will blow and some will fall—
but some will straighten up within His grace
while some will bend to mud, a bitter sprawl.
Repent. His mercy waits for you, divine.
You are His harvest field. Through Him, you shine.

Annabelle Moseley

THE FOURTH LUMINOUS MYSTERY
Fruit of the Mystery:
Courage to Bear the Cross, Desire for Holiness

Raphael
"The Transfiguration"

THE TRANSFIGURATION

We have been given this: the rose-gold glow
of morning on Mount Tabor, torments far
below us. What he wore dazzled like snow.
His face was lightning-splendid as a star.
At first we were stuck in a web of dreams—
woven in sleep by fear, but we awoke
to pristine air, to bright and bridge-like beams
of light anchored to heaven as God spoke.
How much we long to pitch our tents and stay
where everything is luminous and clear.
Our test comes when that vision fades away.
To let our souls transfigure from veneer
to real faith, we must try to stay awake—
for both the glory and the passion's sake.

THE FIFTH LUMINOUS MYSTERY
Fruit of the Mystery:
Greater Love for the Eucharist (Eucharistic Adoration, Active Participation at Mass)

MIRROR SONNET:
MARY DESCRIBES THE INSTITUTION OF THE EUCHARIST

I hoped that when he washed your feet you'd know
how humble he would make himself for love.
How much more will he leave you as he goes?
Food meant to join the earth to God above.
He withholds nothing from you. Take his soul,
his body, blood, divinity within.
Let nothing separate you. He is whole
within you, nourishing—forgiving sin.
He has transfigured, shone his outer view.
He has transformed mere water into wine.
What better wedding gift will he give *you*?
To transubstantiate fruit of the vine,
make work of human hands into what lasts.
He feeds you. But the world would have you fast.

He feeds you. But the world would have you fast.
Make work of human hands into what lasts—
He transubstantiates fruit of the vine.
What better wedding gift could he give you?
He has transformed mere water into wine;
He has transfigured, shone his outer view.
Within you, nourishing—forgiving sin,
let nothing separate you. He is whole.
His body, blood, divinity within,
He withholds nothing from you. Take his soul—
food meant to join the earth to God above.
How much more will he leave you as he goes?
How humble would he make himself for love?
I hoped that when he washed your feet you'd know.

Pontormo
"The Visitation"

Discussion Questions For The Poetry of *Sacred Braille*

Titian
"Madonna in Sorrow"

THE SEVEN SORROWS OF MARY

The Prophecy of Simeon

Choose a line from this poem that speaks to you about the richness of your faith, as seen through the eyes of Mary as she brings her son for a blessing and hears from a prophet about her boy. Which line best sums up the mystery of our faith?

The Flight into Egypt

The definition of "Epiphany" is the manifestation of Christ to the Gentiles through the Three Wise Men, or Magi, whose visit precedes the Flight into Egypt. But in literature and life, an epiphany is defined as a deep, life-changing realization.

What is the epiphany that you've encountered in your faith life and journey? What event gave you clarity regarding what you are being called to do?

The Loss of the Child in the Temple

When in your life did you lose Christ (in big or small ways)? Where did you find Him?

Mary Meets Jesus on the Way of the Cross

What are your favorite prayers or devotions for consoling Mary? Activity: Write your own prayer consoling Mary.

Mary Recalls The Crucifixion

What do you think is the significance of the references to North, South, East, West in this poem? How is this a Sacred Compass?

The Body of Jesus is Prepared for Burial

What are your thoughts and feelings about a broken and vulnerable Christ? What event in Christ's Passion disturbs or pains you most? Explain. What lines in this poem have the greatest impact on you?

Mary Describes the Burial of Jesus

How is it that Christ "nourishes the earth's deep thirst?" What is so poignant about a garden in our faith story?

Fra Angelico
"The Annunciation"

THE JOYFUL MYSTERIES

Mary Remembers The Annunciation

What in Scripture (God's Word) is like a new-formed bud for you? What line in this poem is like hearing the Word in a new and beautiful way, i.e, a bud? When in your life did you "swim into the blessing and the dare" (Stanza 2, line 7)? Explain.

The Visitation

When in your life did you feel that a meeting was more than "chance" and was part of God's plan? Why do you think the poet imagined Elizabeth as the cello, voice strong, and Mary as the viola, a humble inner voice echoing in harmony?

Reflection Activity for The Visitation Mystery – listen to

a classical string quartet as though Elizabeth is the cello, (bass) Mary is the viola (alto) and the babes are the violins (soprano.) All joined in this one embrace.

The Nativity

How is the Birth of Christ like a Calvary, and how is Calvary like a birth? Is there an example in your own life of this understanding?

Mary Recalls the Presentation

Simeon was a messenger of God. Has anyone in your life been a Simeon for you, opening your eyes to the path of faith?

Mary Remembers Finding Jesus in the Temple

Where would you be found and what would you be doing if you were "about your Father's business?"

THE SORROWFUL MYSTERIES

The Agony in the Garden

What in your faith keeps you awake? Have you ever kept someone company in their fear or loneliness? How do you provide "shoots of strength for branch-deep weariness?" Have you ever felt lonely or abandoned when you needed friends during a hard time?

The Scourging of Jesus at the Pillar

"We feel Christ's trembling hand amid the pain./ The whisper of our prayer becomes a call/ to Him, transcending time..." The Rosary allows us, invites us to be present again with Christ in the Mysteries of the Rosary, in His Passion. With your prayers transcending time, what would be your prayer to comfort Christ? Where would you be with Christ as you speak these healing/ loving words to him?

Mirror Sonnet: Jesus is Crowned with Thorns

Though Christ was totally misunderstood, certain acts presented to Him to mock and demean Him, ironically, served as a poignant symbol of His agapic sacrifice and kingship (think cape, crown, words "King of the Jews" hung above His head). But they didn't know what they had done. Which symbolic reference to Christ's identity speaks to your understanding of this the most?

Simon Recalls the Carrying of the Cross

How are you like Simon? How are we all called to be like Simon?

The Crucifixion, Through the Eyes of the Good Thief

When have you experienced a moment of conversion like the Good Thief? Can you think of a time in your life when your eyes were opened by a holy act?

When was your stony heart replaced by one of flesh and blood?

THE GLORIOUS MYSTERIES

Mary Magdalene Describes the Resurrection

How have you experienced answered prayers in the form of a task or a sacred mission? (See stanza 2 lines 2-5)

In this poem we have again a garden reference. This time, Christ is the harvest. Write about or discuss the other garden references in this book, and in Scripture.

The Apostles Recall the Ascension

"Our view/ of heaven's jubilation folds to black/ on our walk home, lonely—wanting you back." Tell of an event or time in your life when letting go was difficult. Were you able to move forward or re-design your life? Or are you still stuck in some way from the loss? If so, how and why? Pray on this theme: The apostles had to feel the Lord's presence in a new way, which empowered them to new action, all while missing Jesus' presence in an earthly way— his voice, his hands.

Peter Describes the Coming of the Holy Spirit

What is the "wind and fire" from God that turns your chalky nature into stone, i.e: a solid rock in the Lord? Is it a talent; your temperament; a transformative event; a person of influence? Has anyone seen something in you that you did not see in yourself? How did you respond to their faith in your abilities? Who are they? What did they see in you?

John Speaks to Mary Before the Assumption

The relationship of John and Blessed Mother as son and mother was "...a gain amidst the loss" (stanza 2 line 4). Holy relationships are life-changing. Contemplating stanza 2, lines 5-6: through whose eyes do you see the face of Christ? If you were to see your heart as an open field, what faith teachings are paramount to your growth in faith? Perhaps a favorite scripture passage, or prayer, or sacrament?

Mary, As She is Crowned

Which line in this poem creates a beautiful image for you of Mary's reunion with her son, and the new knowledge of their mission together, now complete?

Reflection: We have a Mother in Heaven who is also a Queen.

THE LUMINOUS MYSTERIES

The Baptism of Jesus in the River Jordan
The relationship of John the Baptist and Jesus began in the womb and continues into their adulthood. The great John chooses later to decrease so Jesus can increase in his ministry. Jesus humbles himself in this selection, to be baptized by John. This is portrayed in the last 6 lines.

When have you humbled yourself to allow another to fulfill an important task or call? What do you think is meant by: "they met,/ forming a pearl of strength against death's threat"?

To Jesus, At the Wedding Feast at Cana
Were you ever rushed into an important decision when you felt unready? Did someone know you better perhaps than you knew yourself? Or did you act out of love and respect for that person and take something on before you planned? Explain.

Have you ever interpreted the "Wedding Feast" passage in the way described in this poem? How is it that this is also a wedding for Jesus?

The Kingdom of God
What images show the Kingdom of God being "at hand"? What part of the Sermon on the Mount inspires you the most? What would you say is your "call," your "mission"? How did you know? When did it begin like "two stopped clocks"? Did you have a John the Baptist crying out your arrival or inspiring you?

The Transfiguration
Contemplate: Is your faith transfigured or veneer? Is it a living faith? Give examples.

Mirror Sonnet:
Mary Describes The Institution of the Eucharist

The end of Stanza 1 and start of Stanza 2 hold the lines: "He feeds you. But the world would have you fast." What does this convey to you about the contrast between Jesus and the world? Explain.

William-Adolphe Bouguereau
"Madonna of the Roses"

Of Roses and Thorns: A Guided 3-Day Retreat with the Rosary

This retreat may be used for a group over 3 days or can be broken into 1- hour activities over multiple weeks for prayer groups. Another option is to engage this retreat for personal use, for example as a special opportunity for guided prayer during Lent or Advent, to mark a special feast day or just to refresh the soul whenever needed.

Ambrogio Lorenzetti
"The Annunciation"

Evening of the First Day: Intro

When I offer this retreat with groups, I set a table in the front of the classroom or gathering space with an image of Mary's Annunciation as well as a sign which says "YES." This recalls Mary's FIAT, her sacred yes, and reminds us of the "Yes" we are each called to answer God whenever He asks anything of us.

Of course, since we can sometimes fall into the trap of saying "Yes" too often, of being a chronic people pleaser, it is important to distinguish that fiat does not mean self-abuse. Mary is full of grace, gentleness and tenderness... there is no doubt. But she also lived her life with great strength, conviction and let's face it... guts. And she used all of these gifts in the service of the Lord. She was able to stand her ground and do the challenging thing... facing whatever storm crossed her path for the greater glory of God.

Let us look more closely at Mary's Annunciation.

She said "yes" when God asked her help, but that yes did not end with merely agreeing to bear God's only son. Mary's yes continued unfolding, like the petals of a rose, for the rest of her life, and for ever more. Every word and gesture and breath of Mary says "yes" to God. Our lives are meant to be like that. The yes we say to God is not once, it is the Unfolding Yes of our lives.

You have your own Amen, or "So be it," your own "Let it be done unto me," that you are called to give to God. And like a marriage vow, your yes does not end with one promise on one day. It continues to be tested and challenged, as you must each day awaken to renew the consent you gave. The beautiful thing is that every day, each minute is another chance to renew your yes, your sacrifice, to God.

C.S. Lewis said that God plants signs that point to Him in the midst of secular places, so even a pop culture song, for example, can draw souls to Him when they least expect it and in some cases because they do not expect it. Here is a song that was not written with an overtly religious intention and yet it sums up so perfectly the idea of Mary's continuous "yes." Whether we are embarking upon this retreat as an individual or in a group, let us reflect upon what we would like to offer to God as we read the lyrics and listen to the music of the well-known song, "Let it Be" written by Paul McCartney.

(**Play** "Let it Be" and pay extra attention to the lyrics.)

Now read and share reactions to the Preface of this book, which begins on page 13.

We will be looking more closely at the Rosary as a whole but for now let us begin by looking more closely at the Joyful Mysteries.

Note: If doing this retreat as part of a larger prayer or church group, offer each participant a rose. If not a real rose, then give a picture of one. Different color roses should be used so that later people can group together based on rose color for follow-up with group sharing.

Leonardo da Vinci
"The Annunciation"

EVENING OF THE FIRST DAY: THE JOYFUL MYSTERIES

The Annunciation: Read "Mirror Sonnet: The Annunciation" on page 43, view the art on the facing page, then view "The Annunciation" by Fra Angelico.

The Visitation: Read "Visitation Quartet" (page 45), view the art on the facing page, then view "Visitation" by Domenico Ghirlandaio. Think about the strong women you have known who have been true supports to other strong women.

Play Music: "Three Women" by Carrie Newcomber

Journal your gratitude for special women in your life and what women you admire. When was there a visit in your life that was transformative? When did you visit or were visited by others in a life changing way? Why are visits so important/powerful? Imagine what it must have been like when Mary and Elizabeth got together. What did they discuss? What did they share?

Reflection: Listen to a classical string quartet (I recommend any of Haydn's String Quartets Op. 76, Nos. 1, 2 & 3) as though Elizabeth is the cello, (bass) Mary is the viola (alto) and the babes are the violins (soprano.) All are joined in this one embrace. Pray as the music plays and journal the thoughts and feelings that arise.

The Nativity: Read "The Nativity" on page 47, view the art on the facing page, then view "Adoration of the Christ Child" by Coreggio. Journal: Where do you see God's presence in the births of your lives: your own? Your children's? Your family's?

How would you greet the Christ child? What gift would you like to bring him?

The Presentation: First read "Mary Recalls The Presentation" on page 49, view the art on the facing page, then view "Presentation at the Temple" by Bellini.

Mary and Joseph brought the most precious gift of their child to the temple to present him to the Lord because he was a firstborn son and they were following tradition. What gift have you presented to God as dedicated to Him? Is there a tradition, apart from baptism, in your family, that you do to celebrate the birth of a new baby?

When did someone see something special in you, like Simeon and Anna saw?

Journal: What will you present/give/consecrate to God? Your family? Your marriage? Yourself? Your profession? Do so in quiet prayer. If doing as part of a group retreat, have participants write what they present to God on a tag that's on their rose or on the back of the picture of the rose they received. Then bring it up to the altar at Mass on day 3 as part of an offering.

The Finding of Jesus in the Temple: First read "Mary Remembers Finding Jesus in the Temple" on page 51, then view the art on the facing page, then view "Finding Jesus in the Temple" by William Holdman Hunt.

Reflect: When has your faith been lost and then found, if ever? How did you find it? If no one could find YOU where would you say they should have looked? Where are your sacred/special places? When was something that had been lost to you returned to you? Share with a partner or group based on rose color (as mentioned on previous page).

Temple Box Exercise

For this exercise, get a small decorative or simple box and in it place little pieces of paper, each one with a virtue written on it. Fold each in half; have group (or yourself, if taking this retreat alone) pick one out of this box as a "finding." Trust that God has allowed you to find this today; a certain good sent by Him that he knows you need.

Journal: What has God helped you to find when it was lost?

If time allows: Two of the Same Roses

Once again, find a person who has the same color rose that you do. If you do not have a partner, presenter will be your partner. Visit with each other like Mary and Elizabeth. Share with each other: What is a blessing in your life you need to celebrate right now? What is a burden in your life right now that needs prayer?

Share tea, coffee, cookies

End with Prayer

MORNING OF THE SECOND DAY: THE LUMINOUS MYSTERIES

In the light of a new day, let us begin the luminous mysteries.

The Baptism of Christ: First read "The Baptism of Jesus in the River Jordan" on page 79 and view the art on the facing page, then view "The Baptism of Jesus Christ" by Tintoretto.

What details of your baptism do you know? Godparents' names? Church name? Patron saint? Priest? How it was celebrated? Details you were told? Your children's baptisms? This helps to craft your spiritual autobiography.

The Wedding Feast at Cana: First read "To Jesus, At The Wedding Feast at Cana" on page 81 and view the art on the facing page, then view "Wedding at Cana" by Duccio.

The "Yes" of marriage is a joyful and beautiful sacrifice: roses and thorns. Look how Jesus has blessed the institution of marriage. How very blessed the sacrament of marriage is that it was named by John the Evangelist as the very first Sign of Jesus. In a marriage, the everyday offerings and sacrifices we make (the water, if you will) are transformed over time into sacred wine when we raise up the ordinary standards of commitment to the extraordinary standards of a marriage that invites Christ to its center. And now we see that this act, at first glance over a small matter as a wine shortage, becomes very great indeed. Let us, in our marriages, offer the vessels of water up to Christ, on a daily basis, to be turned into holy wine. And as holy wine, the best that wine can offer in its good uses: enjoyment, relaxation, celebration, sharing, peace, and an inebriation of love.

This miracle of water turned into wine is a wonderful foreshadowing of the even greater miracle of the Last Supper and the Institution of the Eucharist. If Christ is willing to transform water into wine at the Wedding of Cana, how much more willing is He to transform mere bread and wine into His sacred self, broken and shared for us? After all, he said that he would not leave us orphans. He is physically absent from us after his Ascension but he gives the Holy Spirit to comfort and guide us and the Eucharist to sustain and transform us.

Did you ever do something great that you were not ready to do, but trusted the encouragement of a loved one?

Tell of a time when you longed for Eucharist to sustain you through a difficult time.

The Proclamation of the Kingdom: First read "The Kingdom of God" on page 83 and view the art on the facing page, then view "The Proclamation of the Kingdom of God" by Fra Angelico.

The Beatitudes were given so we can be happy. Read the Beatitudes and journal which one you need to draw upon most in your life this year, so you can be more happy.

The Transfiguration: First read "The Transfiguration" on page 85 and view the art on the facing page, then view "The Transfiguration" by Fra Angelico.

Much like the mountain in scripture, where is a sacred place besides Church to which you retreat?

Have you ever felt in some way transfigured by God?

Jesus Institutes the Eucharist: First, read "Mirror Sonnet: Mary Describes the Institution of the Eucharist" on page 87 and view the art on the facing page, which depicts a self-sacrificial symbol from Medieval Christianity and Catholic art known as "The Pelican in her Piety." The mother bird wounds herself to feed her own blood to her starving chicks in a process known as "vulning" (the word vulnerable comes from the same Latin root meaning "to wound"). Answer this: Has anyone in your own life loved you like that? Then view "The Institution of the Eucharist" by Fra Angelico and "Our Lady of the Most Blessed Sacrament" by Jean Auguste Dominique Ingres.

Jean Auguste Dominique Ingres
"The Virgin of the Host"

AFTERNOON OF THE SECOND DAY: THE SORROWFUL MYSTERIES

Promptly begin at 1:00

Begin by journaling: What are the sorrowful mysteries in your life, the challenges you don't fully understand but that you can offer up to God?

The Agony in the Garden: First read "The Agony in the Garden" on page 55 and view the art on the facing page, then view "Agony in the Garden" by Bellini.

Read the scripture for "The Agony in the Garden" (page 111), and follow the four steps of *Lectio Divina* as detailed starting on page 137.

What word or line touches you the most? Why? Share or journal.

When have you been friendless or lonely in the midst of suffering?

Have you ever kept watch through the night over an elderly parent, infirm relative, or a new baby? Where you aware of Christ's presence at the time, or some time later? Share.

Now **journal**: How can we stay awake with Jesus in Gethsemane?

We contemplate this as we pray the **"Golden Arrow"** prayer together as was dictated by Our Lord to Sister Mary of St. Peter:

May the most holy, most sacred, most adorable, most incomprehensible and unutterable Name of God be always praised, blessed, loved, adored and glorified, in Heaven, on earth, and under the earth, by all the creatures of God, and by the Sacred Heart of Our Lord Jesus Christ in the Most Holy Sacrament of the Altar. Amen.

Let's resolve to stay awake with Him in the Garden. We can do this because God is outside of time and space.

What are good ways to stay awake with Him?

- Mass
- Holy Hour
- Praying to the Holy Face
- Praying the Sorrowful Mysteries of the Rosary
- Add your own

Journal: How do you purpose to do this more?

As participants journal, play Song: "To Make You Feel My Love" sung by Garth Brooks.

Group Activity: have participants break into groups of two, to share with each other a sorrow they would like the other person to pray for. Resolve to "keep each other company" by continuing to pray for each other going forward.

Fra Angelico
"Lamentation over Christ"

Lectio Divina Exercise: The Agony in the Garden. (MT 26:36-46)

36 Then Jesus came with them to a place called Gethsemane, and he said to his disciples, "Sit here while I go over there and pray."

37 He took along Peter and the two sons of Zebedee, and began to feel sorrow and distress.

38 Then he said to them, "My soul is sorrowful even to death. Remain here and keep watch with me."

39 He advanced a little and fell prostrate in prayer, saying, "My Father, if it is possible, let this cup pass from me; yet, not as I will, but as you will."

40 When he returned to his disciples he found them asleep. He said to Peter, "So you could not keep watch with me for one hour?

41 Watch and pray that you may not undergo the test. The spirit is willing, but the flesh is weak."

42 Withdrawing a second time, he prayed again, "My Father, if it is not possible that this cup pass without my drinking it, your will be done!"

43 Then he returned once more and found them asleep, for they could not keep their eyes open.

44 He left them and withdrew again and prayed a third time, saying the same thing again.

45 Then he returned to his disciples and said to them, "Are you still sleeping and taking your rest? Behold, the hour is at hand when the Son of Man is to be handed over to sinners.

46 "Get up, let us go. Look, my betrayer is at hand."

The Scourging at the Pillar: First read "The Scourging of Jesus at the Pillar" on page 57, and view the accompanying art.

As we dwell prayerfully with the Second Sorrowful Mystery, The

Scourging of Jesus at the Pillar, let us view a work of art called "The Flagellation of Christ" by Caravaggio painted in 1607.

The Crowning With Thorns: First read "Mirror Sonnet: Jesus is Crowned With Thorns" on page 59 along with the accompanying art, then view "The Crowning with Thorns" by Caravaggio.

By the way, Jesus' cloak reminds a bit of the cloak Joseph was mocked for by his brothers.

Look on a red rose and don't just see Mary. See Christ. There is the cloak that was cast around him and there are the thorns. Look what beauty he made of it! What can you make of the burdensome cape around you, the ways you've been mocked, the thorns you have felt? What can you do with them?

In keeping with the theme of Christ being crowned with thorns and wounded, mocked, and tortured; and in keeping with the artistic genius of Fra Angelico who paints poetically, his canvas filled with symbolic colors and images... treat yourself to viewing the unforgettable "Mocking of Christ" by Fra Angelico, and I daresay the very first glimpse of the image will move you to prayer.

It was created in 1440 by Fra Angelico on the wall of Cell 7 in Convento di San Marco in Florence. This was a painting by a monk for his brother monks as a tool to increase the devotion of their prayers. This painting is genius in its depiction of mockery of our Lord and of blasphemy as the face of Christ is spat upon and slapped. In the words of St. Catherine of Siena, "May any man be ashamed to raise his head in pride, seeing you, Highest Lord, humiliated on the side of our humanity."

In a humble spirit of love and reparation we pause to pray now the Golden Arrow Prayer in honor of the Holy Face of Jesus. (see **Golden Arrow Prayer** on page 109)

The Carrying of the Cross: First read "Simon Recalls the Carrying of the Cross" on page 61 and view the art on the facing page, then view "The Carrying of the Cross" by El Greco.

Distribute the lyrics to "Shoulders" by For King and Country. Pay special attention to the lyrics and underline any line or word that especially touches you, as with *Lectio Divina*.

Now play the song. Then **journal**: Imagine the shoulders of Christ. What pain of yours does he carry on them? Take this opportunity to ask him to receive your burden and to thank him for all he carries for you.

In this world, become Simon. Allow someone else to be Simon for you. Good parents do it all the time, carrying burdens of their children.

The Crucifixion: First read "The Crucifixion, Through the Eyes of the Good Thief" on page 63 and view the art on the facing page, then view "The Crucifixion" by Andrea del Castagno.

Here are the seven last words (phrases, sayings) of Christ:

1. Father, forgive them; for they know not what they do.
2. Today you will be with me in Paradise.
3. Woman, behold thy son! Son, behold, thy mother.
4. My God, my God, why hast thou forsaken me?
5. I thirst.
6. It is finished.
7. Father, into thy hands I commend my spirit.

Now play Haydn's "Seven Last Words of Christ". Which last word of Christ do you need the most now?

Distribute lyrics to "All of Me" by Matt Hammitt and play song.

Journal: About giving your whole self to God- what do you want to give, what is hard to give, what is effortless to give, how do you feel as you give it, how do you hope Christ will feel as he receives it? How do you want to love him?

Pray this short aspiration: "Jesus, remember me when you come into your kingdom."

2:00: If doing a group retreat, Discuss Divine Mercy Hour and Divine Mercy Sunday. After all, Mary wants greater awareness of her son's great mercy.

Give handouts on Divine Mercy or show a film on the subject for 30 minutes, telling them you will signal when it is time to go to Quiet Session. If doing this retreat as your own immersion, use the time to meditate on Divine Mercy.

2:30: Quiet Session (If doing with retreat, perhaps you could arrange with a priest for Reconciliation to be available).

3:00: Divine Mercy Hour (If doing with retreat, perhaps you could arrange with a priest for Eucharistic Adoration to be available.)

Pray the Divine Mercy chaplet (page 115) and consider how every challenging opportunity in our lives offers us a chance to stay awake with Jesus in Gethsemane, keeping him company there.

2:30-4:00: rest, silent time, quiet prayer, reflection, nap, or nature walk.

Please be back promptly at 4:00 to begin the Glorious Mysteries.

HONORING THE FIFTH SORROWFUL MYSTERY THROUGH THE DIVINE MERCY CHAPLET:

1. Make the Sign of the Cross
In the name of the Father, and of the Son, and of the Holy Spirit. Amen.

2. Optional Opening Prayers
You expired, Jesus, but the source of life gushed forth for souls, and the ocean of mercy opened up for the whole world. O Fount of Life, unfathomable Divine Mercy, envelop the whole world and empty Yourself out upon us.

(Repeat three times)

O Blood and Water, which gushed forth from the Heart of Jesus as a fount of mercy for us, I trust in You!

3. Our Father
Our Father, Who art in heaven, hallowed be Thy name; Thy kingdom come; Thy will be done on earth as it is in heaven. Give us this day our daily bread; and forgive us our trespasses as we forgive those who trespass against us; and lead us not into temptation, but deliver us from evil, Amen.

4. Hail Mary
Hail Mary, full of grace. The Lord is with thee. Blessed art thou amongst women, and blessed is the fruit of thy womb, Jesus. Holy Mary, Mother of God, pray for us sinners, now and at the hour of our death, Amen.

5. The Apostles' Creed
I believe in God, the Father almighty, Creator of heaven and earth, and in Jesus Christ, His only Son, our Lord, who was conceived by

the Holy Spirit, born of the Virgin Mary, suffered under Pontius Pilate, was crucified, died and was buried; He descended into hell; on the third day He rose again from the dead; He ascended into heaven, and is seated at the right hand of God the Father almighty; from there He will come to judge the living and the dead. I believe in the Holy Spirit, the holy Catholic Church, the communion of saints, the forgiveness of sins, the resurrection of the body, and life everlasting. Amen.

6. **The Eternal Father**
Eternal Father, I offer you the Body and Blood, Soul and Divinity of Your Dearly Beloved Son, Our Lord, Jesus Christ, in atonement for our sins and those of the whole world.

7. **On the 10 Small Beads of Each Decade**
For the sake of His sorrowful Passion, have mercy on us and on the whole world.

8. **Repeat for the remaining decades**
Saying the "Eternal Father" on the "Our Father" bead and then 10 "For the sake of His sorrowful Passion" on the following "Hail Mary" beads.

9. **Conclude with Holy God** (Repeat three times)
Holy God, Holy Mighty One, Holy Immortal One, have mercy on us and on the whole world.

10. **Optional Closing Prayer**
Eternal God, in whom mercy is endless and the treasury of compassion — inexhaustible, look kindly upon us and increase Your mercy in us, that in difficult moments we might not despair nor become despondent, but with great confidence submit ourselves to Your holy will, which is Love and Mercy itself.

AFTERNOON OF THE SECOND DAY:
THE GLORIOUS MYSTERIES

Begin promptly at 4:00

The Resurrection: First read "Mary Magdelene Describes the Resurrection" on page 67 and view the art on the facing page, then view "Christ's Appearance to Mary Magdalene After the Resurrection" by Alexander Ivanov.

When have resurrections appeared in the wake of your life's sorrows?

The Ascension: First read "The Apostles Recall the Ascension" on page 69, view the art on the facing page, then view "The Ascension" by Giotto.

The Descent of the Holy Spirit: First read "Peter Describes the Coming of the Holy Spirit" on page 71, view the art on the facing page, then view "Descent of Holy Spirit on the Apostles" by Mikhail Vrubel.

View the lyrics to "Soul on Fire" by Third Day, then play song. Pick your favorite line or word, and journal.

The Assumption: First read "John Speaks to Mary before the Assumption" on page 73, view the art on the facing page, then view "The Assumption" by El Greco.

The Crowning of Mary: First read "Mary, As She is Crowned" on page 75, then view "Coronation of the Virgin" by Fra Filippo Lippi.

"I'd do it all again" Meditation: In the poem, Mary states that she would go through all the pain again to say yes to God. What would you do again, even though it was hard, to say yes to God?

Pray Full Rosary: The Glorious Mysteries

EVENING OF THE SECOND DAY

Dress for Mass (if a Saturday evening) or Prayer Service and Supper.

Mass or Prayer Service Supper Group Activity:
Plan a meal with your prayer or retreat group (even if it's a simple repast of bread, grapes and cheese), or with friends or family. First, say Grace before meals. If you are comfortable, it might be nice to hold hands with each other, or hold your hands open in a gesture of welcoming God and neighbor.

As you break bread, please take turns (one at a time in a circle) telling the other people at your table about an object you have in your home (either in your kitchen or dining room) that holds a special meaning for you. For example: A serving tray your grandmother used, candlesticks from your wedding, a statue or picture. Explain the symbolism of this object, how it enhances the beauty or sense of meaning in your domestic church, where your own feasts and suppers take place.

8:15 Prepare for Evening Prayer

8:30 Closing Evening Prayer

Recite the Litany of Loreto (by candlelight)

Play (and if comfortable, join in singing) "Mary Did You Know?" by Kathy Mattea.

Recite The Memorare

Say Compline Prayers, extinguish candles, and head to bed.

Morning of the Third Day:
Sorrows and Un-tied Knots

9:30 Morning Session: Mary, Untier of Knots

Read The Seven Sorrows of Mary poems (pages 27 to 39), along with the accompanying art.

10:30: Aware of Mary's Sorrows, we bring her ours as we approach the great Untier of Knots.

Journal: What knots would you like to bring to Mary?

Johann Georg Melchior
Schmidtner
"Mary, Untier of Knots"

Have each participant write down their knot, and fold it up, then tie a string of yarn around the paper and one at a time, place before a statue of Mary at the front of the room. As they place their knotted prayer, let them take away the gift of a Rosary, each wrapped and waiting in a bowl next to the Mary statue. Now the participants have exchanged their knots for the way to unbind them: through praying the Rosary!

Play beautiful, sacred music: such as Pavarotti's "Ave Maria", and pray quietly.

Have participants now open Rosary beads.

12:00: Noon Departure

William-Adolphe Bouguereau
"Madonna of the Lilies"

Giovanni Bellini
"Alzano Madonna"

COMPONENTS OF THE ROSARY

A Sacred Palette for Praying a Masterpiece

Some like to say an Act of Contrition prior to the Rosary:

ACT OF CONTRITION

O my God, I am heartily sorry for having offended Thee, and I detest all my sins because of Thy just punishments, but most of all because they offend Thee, my God, Who art all-good and deserving of all my love. I firmly resolve, with the help of Thy grace, to sin no more and to avoid the near occasions of sin.

HOW TO PRAY THE ROSARY

- Make the Sign of the Cross.
- Holding the Crucifix, say the Preparatory Prayer and then the Apostles' Creed.
- On the first bead, say an Our Father.
- Say one Hail Mary on each of the next three beads.
- Say the Glory Be.
- As you begin each of the five decades, state the Mystery. You may then wish to read a corresponding Scripture passage.
- Then say the Our Father.
- While touching each of the ten beads of the decade, next pray ten Hail Marys while meditating on the Mystery.
- Then pray a Glory Be.

(After finishing each decade, some say the following prayer requested by the Blessed Virgin Mary at Fatima: O my Jesus, forgive us our sins, save us from the fires of hell; lead all souls to Heaven, especially those who have most need of your mercy.)

PRAYERS OF THE ROSARY

Preparatory Prayer

O God, come to my assistance. O Lord, make haste to help me. In the name of the Father, Son, and Holy Spirit, Amen. Glory be to the Father, and to the Son and to the Holy Spirit, as it was in the beginning, is now, and ever shall be, world without end. Amen.

The Apostles' Creed

I believe in God, the Father Almighty, Creator of heaven and earth; and in Jesus Christ, His only Son, our Lord; Who was conceived by the Holy Spirit, born of the Virgin Mary, suffered under Pontius Pilate, was crucified, died and was buried. He descended into hell; on the third day He rose again from the dead; He ascended into heaven, where He sits at the right hand of God, the Father Almighty; from thence He shall come to judge the living and the dead. I believe in the Holy Spirit, the holy Catholic Church, the communion of saints, the forgiveness of sins, the resurrection of the body, and life everlasting. Amen.

The Lord's Prayer (Our Father)

Our Father, Who art in Heaven, hallowed be Thy name; Thy Kingdom come, Thy will be done on earth as it is in Heaven. Give us this day our daily bread; and forgive us our trespasses as we forgive those who trespass against us; and lead us not into temptation, but deliver us from evil. Amen.

Then pray Three Hail Marys:

- For the gift of Faith
- For the gift of Hope
- For the gift of Charity (Love)

Hail Mary
Hail Mary, full of grace, the Lord is with thee. Blessed art thou among women, and blessed is the fruit of thy womb, Jesus. Holy Mary, Mother of God, pray for us sinners, now and at the hour of our death. Amen.

Glory Be
Glory be to the Father, and to the Son, and to the Holy Spirit, as it was in the beginning, is now, and ever shall be, world without end. Amen.

O My Jesus (Fatima Prayer)
O my Jesus, forgive us our sins, save us from the fires of hell, and lead all souls to heaven, especially those in most need of thy mercy. Amen.

After you say the five decades of the Rosary dwelling on each mystery, (1 Our Father, 10 Hail Marys, 1 Glory Be and 1 O My Jesus per decade) say the Hail, Holy Queen (Salve Regina), followed by this dialogue and prayer:

Salve Regina
Hail Holy Queen, Mother of mercy; hail, our life, our sweetness, and our hope. To you do we cry, poor banished children of Eve; to you do we send up our sighs, mourning and weeping in this valley of tears. Turn then, most gracious advocate, thine eyes of mercy towards us; and after this our exile, show unto us the blessed Fruit of thy womb, Jesus: O clement, O loving, O sweet Virgin Mary!

(Verse) Pray for us, O Holy Mother of God.

(Response) That we may be made worthy of the promises of Christ.

Concluding Rosary Prayer

(Verse) Let us pray,

(Response) O God, whose only begotten Son, by His life, death, and resurrection, has purchased for us the rewards of eternal salvation. Grant, we beseech Thee, that while meditating on these mysteries of the most holy Rosary of the Blessed Virgin Mary, that we may both imitate what they contain and obtain what they promise, through Christ our Lord. Amen.

Most Sacred Heart of Jesus, have mercy on us.

Immaculate Heart of Mary, pray for us.

Some like to then pray this **Prayer to Saint Michael the Archangel**:

Saint Michael the Archangel, defend us in battle. Be our protection against the wickedness and snares of the devil; May God rebuke him, we humbly pray; And do thou, O Prince of the Heavenly Host, by the power of God, thrust into hell Satan and all evil spirits who wander through the world for the ruin of souls. Amen.

* * *

To pray the Holy Rosary along with author Annabelle Moseley, featuring Sacred Braille art and poetic reflections on the Mysteries, visit **www.annabellemoseley.com/rosary/**

Giovanni Bellini
"Madonna of the Meadow"

Leonardo da Vinci
"Virgin and Child with St. Anne"

15 ROSARY PROMISES

From Mary to Those Who Who Say the Rosary
Daily, as Told by St. Dominic

1. To all those who shall pray my Rosary devoutly, I promise my special protection and great graces.

2. Those who shall persevere in the recitation of my Rosary will receive some special grace.

3. The Rosary will be a very powerful armor against hell; it will destroy vice, deliver from sin and dispel heresy.

4. The Rosary will make virtue and good works flourish, and will obtain for souls the most abundant divine mercies. It will draw the hearts of men from the love of the world and its vanities, and will lift them to the desire of eternal things. Oh, that souls would sanctify themselves by this means.

5. Those who trust themselves to me through the Rosary will not perish.

6. Whoever recites my Rosary devoutly reflecting on the mysteries, shall never be overwhelmed by misfortune. He will not experience the anger of God nor will he perish by an unprovided death. The sinner will be converted; the just will persevere in grace and merit eternal life.

7. Those truly devoted to my Rosary shall not die without the sacraments of the Church.

8. Those who are faithful to recite my Rosary shall have during their life and at their death the light of God and the plenitude of His graces and will share in the merits of the blessed.

9. I will deliver promptly from purgatory souls devoted to my Rosary.

10. True children of my Rosary will enjoy great glory in heaven.

11. What you shall ask through my Rosary you shall obtain.

12. To those who propagate my Rosary I promise aid in all their necessities.

13. I have obtained from my Son that all the members of the Rosary Confraternity shall have as their intercessors, in life and in death, the entire celestial court.

14. Those who recite my Rosary faithfully are my beloved children, the brothers and sisters of Jesus Christ.

15. Devotion to my Rosary is a special sign of predestination.

Consider joining the Rosary Confraternity if you are able to commit to praying the Rosary at least three times a week. It aligns your prayers to all the other members of the confraternity and vice-versa.

Learn more at rosarycenter.org by clicking the "Confraternity" tab on the homepage.

"If anyone has the happiness of being in the Confraternity of the Rosary, he has in all corners of the world brothers and sisters who pray for him."

-Cure of Ars

Fra Angelico
"Sacred Conversation"

Sandro Botticelli
"Cestello Annunciation"

Michelangelo
"Pieta"

VISIO DIVINA WITH EACH MYSTERY OF THE ROSARY

More Great Works of Art Recommended to View for Each Mystery of the Rosary

Visio Divina translates to "Divine Seeing" or "Sacred Seeing." This ancient form of prayer allows us to pray with "the eyes of the heart." Allow yourself to enter the work of art, to dwell with it and within it until it becomes illuminated with deeper meaning for your own prayer life.

Here are images worth searching for, gazing upon and dwelling deeply among. Perhaps you'll find a favorite to purchase as a print and frame in your own domestic church.

THE SEVEN SORROWS OF MARY

The Prophecy of Simeon: "Simeon the Righteous" by Alexei Egorov

The Flight into Egypt: "Flight into Egypt" by George Hitchcock

The Loss of the Child Jesus in the Temple: "Christ Among the Doctors" by Paolo Veronese

The Meeting of Jesus and Mary on The Way of the Cross: "Christ Meets His Mother" by Caravaggio

The Crucifixion: "Crucifixion" by Josse Lieferinxe

The Taking Down of the Body of Jesus from the Cross: "Pieta" by Michelangelo

The Burial of Jesus: "The Burial of Christ" by Francisco Goya, "The Entombment" by Garofalo (Benvenuto Tisi)

The Joyful Mysteries

The Annunciation: "The Annunciation" by Jacopo Tintoretto, "Ecce Ancilla Domini!" by Dante Gabriel Rossetti, "The Annunciation" by Henry Ossawa Tanner

The Visitation: "Visitation" by Raphael, "Visitation" by Ghirlandaio, "The Visitation" by Henry Ossawa Tanner

The Nativity: "Adoration of the Magi" by Ghirlandaio, "Adoration of the Shepherds" by Gerard van Honthorst, "The Nativity" by Edward Burne-Jones, "The Adoration of the Magi" by Gentile da Fabriano

The Presentation: "Presentation at the Temple" by Giovanni Bellini, "The Presentation of Jesus in the Temple" 1627 by Rembrandt van Rijn

The Finding of Jesus in the Temple: "Jesus Found in the Temple, illustration for The Life of Christ" by James Tissot, "The Finding of the Saviour in the Temple" by William Holman Hunt

The Sorrowful Mysteries

The Agony in the Garden: "The Agony in the Garden" 1457-1459 by Andrea Mantegna, "The Agony in the Garden" by Heinrich Hofmann

The Scourging at the Pillar: "Flagellation of Christ" by Rubens, "The Scourging at the Pillar" by William-Adolphe Bouguereau

Jesus Is Crowned With Thorns: "Christ Crowned with Thorns" by Fra Angelico, "The Crowning with Thorns" by Caravaggio, "Christ Crowned with Thorns" by Maarten van Heemskerck

The Carrying of the Cross: "Christ Carrying the Cross" by El Greco, "Christ Bearing the Cross by Lorenzo Lotto

The Crucifixion: "Christ of St John of the Cross" by Salvador Dali, "Cristo Crucificado" by Diego Velázquez

THE GLORIOUS MYSTERIES

The Resurrection: "Christ and Mary Magdalene" (Noli me tangere) by Titian, "The Incredulity of St. Thomas" by Caravaggio

The Ascension: "Ascension (Scrovegni Chapel)" by Giotto, "Ascension" by Andrea Mantegna, "Ascension" by Garofalo

The Descent of the Holy Spirit: "The Descent of the Holy Spirit" by Tiziano Vecellio 1545, "Pentecost" by Giovanni Lanfranco, 1630

The Assumption of Mary: "Assumption of the Virgin" by Rubens, "Assumption" by Annibale Carraci, "Assumption of the Virgin Fresco" (Parma Cathedral) by Antonio da Correggio, "Assumption" by Mateo Cerezo

The Coronation of Mary: "Coronation of the Virgin" by Diego Velazquez, "Paradise" (dome frescoes, Baptistry, Padua) 1375-76 by Giusto de Menabuoi

THE LUMINOUS MYSTERIES

The Baptism of Jesus in the River Jordan: "The Baptism of Christ" by Piero della Francesca

The Wedding Feast at Cana: "Wedding Feast at Cana" by Duccio, "The Wedding Feast at Cana" by Julius Schnorr von Carolsfeld

Jesus Proclaims the Kingdom of God: "Sermon on the Mount" by Carl Bloch

The Transfiguration of Jesus: "The Transfiguration" by Giovanni Bellini, "Transfiguration" by Alexandr Ivanov

Jesus Institutes the Eucharist: "The Last Supper" by Fra Angelico, "The Last Supper" by Leonardo da Vinci, "The Last Supper" by Salvador Dali

LECTIO DIVINA WITH EACH MYSTERY OF THE ROSARY

One option while praying the Rosary is to meditate upon a line or two from a related Scripture passage with each "Hail Mary" or for the mystery as a whole.

THE FOUR STEPS OF LECTIO DIVINA

1. **Lectio**, or Read the passage of Scripture. This stage is also known as "Listening."
2. Then, **Meditatio**, or Meditate which is the phase of ruminating on Sacred Scripture with the famous image of the animal silently chewing his cud, turning the Word over and over as we memorize it and it becomes part of us, as we repeat it to ourselves and let the Word engage our soul. So you first read the text, then reflect on it.
3. The third step is **Oratio**, or Pray. St. Ambrose said, "And let them remember that prayer should accompany the reading of Sacred Scripture, so that God and man may talk together; for "we speak to Him when we pray; we hear Him when we read the divine saying."
4. **Contemplatio**, or Contemplate. For this step, it is important to think deeply while sitting in slience.

Here is a Mnemonic device I devised for my Graduate Theology students to remember the steps for *Lectio Divina* in order of how they are meant to be followed: **Lead Me O Christ**

Lectio, **M**editatio, **O**ratio, **C**ontemplatio. Using the four steps of *Lectio Divina*, read; meditate; pray; and contemplate on the reading.

Another option: Meditate while saying the Rosary not just on the words you are praying, but on an image from the reading of scripture. This helps to focus. For example, for the Luminous Mysteries, at "The Wedding at Cana," you may picture water flowing into a jar, turning into wine as it pours.

During the "Baptism of Jesus" imagine the light on the Jordan River, and the Baptist squinting in the sunlight, as Jesus approaches in all that brightness. When Jesus states at The Proclamation of the Kingdom of God, "The kingdom of God is at hand," imagine his beautiful hands. They are still un-pierced; they have no wounds at this point. Imagine what they look like there, and how they will change for us. If you are having trouble focusing, look down at your own hands and vow to use them for good this day. (Have a meditation on image section and do one for each mystery.) Here are some suggested scripture for each mystery and sorrow.

The Seven Sorrows of Mary

The Prophecy of Simeon: Lk 2:34-35
The Flight into Egypt: Mt 2:13-14
The Loss of the Child in the Temple: Lk 2:43-45
The Meeting of Jesus and Mary on The Way of the Cross: Lk 23:27
The Crucifixion: Jn 19:25-27
The taking down of the Body of Jesus from the Cross: Mk 15:43-46
The Burial of Jesus: Jn 19:41-42

The Joyful Mysteries

The Annunciation: Lk 1:26-38
The Visitation: Lk 1:39-49
The Nativity: Lk 2:6-12
The Presentation: Lk 2:22-35
The Finding of Jesus in the Temple: Lk 2:41-51

The Sorrowful Mysteries

The Agony in the Garden: Lk 22:43-44
The Scourging at the Pillar: Mk 15:15

Jesus Is Crowned With Thorns: Mt 27:27-31
The Carrying of the Cross: Lk 23:26
The Crucifixion: Jn 19:25-27

THE GLORIOUS MYSTERIES

The Resurrection: Mt 28:1-6
The Ascension: Lk 24:36-51
The Descent of the Holy Spirit: Acts 2:1-4
The Assumption of Virgin Mary into Heaven:
Jdt 13:18- 20; Jdt 15:10; 1Chr 15; 1Chr 16; Psa 45; Psa 132
The Coronation of Mary: Rev 12:1

THE LUMINOUS MYSTERIES

The Baptism of Jesus in the River Jordan: Mt 3:13-17
The Wedding Feast at Cana: Jn 2:1-12
Jesus Proclaims the Kingdom of God: Mk 1:15
The Transfiguration of Jesus: Lk 9:28-35
Jesus Institutes the Eucharist: Mk 14:22-25

John William Waterhouse, "The Annunciation"

William-Adolphe Bouguereau
"Song of the Angels"

Audio Divina with Each Mystery of the Rosary

Another option while praying the Rosary is to meditate on music chosen for its connection to the mysteries. You'll find here a blend of both sacred and secular music, to increase the variety of places we can encounter God. It is fascinating and moving to hear a secular song that might as well have been written for a particular mystery. There are also famous hymns and classical music that are time-honored genius, as transformative to the soul as a Bernini sculpture or Shakespearean sonnet. Playing one of these songs prior to saying the prayers of that particular mystery can deeply enhance one's emotional connection to the subject.

The Seven Sorrows of Mary

The Prophecy of Simeon: "Now That I've Held Him in My Arms" by Michael Card

The Flight into Egypt: "The Flight into Egypt" by Nightnoise (meditative instrumental)

The Loss of the Child in the Temple: "You Were There" by Libera, "Who You Say I Am" by Hillsong Worship, "In My Father's House" (church hymn)

Mary Meets Jesus on The Way of the Cross: "Stabat Mater, RV 621", by Antonio Vivaldi

The Crucifixion: St. Matthew Passion by Bach, Messiah by Handel, "Adagio for Strings" by Samuel Barber

The Preparation of Jesus' Body for Burial: "Ave Maria" by Luciano Pavarotti

Mirror Sonnet:The Burial of Jesus: "Thy Will" by Hillary Scott and the Scott Family

THE JOYFUL MYSTERIES

The Annunciation: "Let it Be" by The Beatles, "Be Born in Me" by Francesca Battistelli

The Visitation: "Magnificat" by Bach, "Three Women" by Carrie Newcomber

The Nativity: "A New Day Has Come" by Celine Dion
The Presentation: "Breath of Heaven" by Melissa Manchester

The Finding of Jesus in the Temple: "That's the Way it Is" by Celine Dion

THE SORROWFUL MYSTERIES

The Agony in the Garden: "To Make You Feel My Love" by Garth Brooks

The Scourging at the Pillar: "Mary Did You Know" by Kathy Mattea

Jesus Is Crowned With Thorns: "O Sacred Head Now Wounded" hymn

Simon Recalls the Carrying of the Cross: "Shoulders" by For King & Country, "Brother" by Need to Breathe featuring Gavin deGraw, "Parsifal Act III" by Wagner

The Crucifixion, Through The Eyes of The Good Thief: "All of Me" by Matt Hammitt, "Seven Last Words of Christ" Haydn, "Where My Father Lives" hymn

THE GLORIOUS MYSTERIES

The Resurrection: Symphony No. 2 ('Resurrection') – Mahler and "Scars" by I Am They

The Apostles Recall The Ascension: "Soon and Very Soon" (We are Going to See the King) by Andrae Crouch

Peter Describes The Coming of the Holy Spirit:
"Soul on Fire" by Third Day

The Assumption of Mary: "How Great Thou Art"

The Coronation of Mary: "Mother and Child Reunion" by
Paul Simon

THE LUMINOUS MYSTERIES

The Baptism of Jesus in the River Jordan: "The Litany of
Saints" by John Becker

The Wedding Feast at Cana: Jesus Addresses the Servers:
"Everything I Do (I Do It For You)" by Bryan Adams

Jesus Proclaims the Kingdom of God: "You Say" by
Lauren Daigle

The Transfiguration of Jesus: "Transfigure Us, O God" Hymn

Jesus Institutes the Eucharist: "See You in the Eucharist" by
Danielle Rose

Caravaggio, "Rest on the Flight Into Egypt"

Caravaggio
"Madonna of the Rosary"

A Living Rosary

Here's a suggestion for a special and memorable way to pray the Rosary in community. Try a Living Rosary! There are two main ways to do it. One is the way that Pope Saint John Paul II loved. He was not only a member, but also an advocate for Living Rosary prayer groups.

The Living Rosary as a devotion began in 1826 in France. That's when Venerable Pauline-Marie Jaricot founded the Living Rosary Association. She organized groups of 15 individuals who would each be responsible for praying one Rosary decade per day. In this way, the complete 15-decade Rosary would be prayed daily by the group, through their combined efforts.

> *After Our Lady of the Rosary, the Association recognizes and honors as its mediatrix before God, the illustrious Virgin and Martyr, St. Philomena, named by the Sovereign Pontiff, protectress of the Living Rosary."*
> — Venerable Pauline–Marie Jaricot

Over a century later, Karol Wotylwa—the young St. John Paul II (who would later introduce the Luminous Mysteries in his pontificate) came to love the Living Rosary devotion.

Purpose of the Universal Living Rosary Association

> *"The aim of the Living Rosary is to ask God, through the intercession of Our Lady of the Rosary, for the conservation of the Faith in Catholic countries, the conversion of sinners, the strengthening of the just, and the exaltation of the Holy Church.*

The people who join together for this pious exercise, divide among themselves the recitation of the prayers of the entire Rosary, and divide into groups of 15, in honor of the 15 principal mysteries of our redemption. Their intention is to form, by the union of their hearts, as so many living rosaries which unceasingly recall to the Celestial Father the sign of salvation manifested to St. Dominic by the Mother of Mercies."
—The Universal Living Rosary Association
of Saint Philomena

Looking for a special way to pray the Rosary? Try bringing a Living Rosary to your school, church, home, Rosary society, or religious community. You can try doing the Living Rosary as suggested above, the way Pope Saint John Paul II prayed it. Or, you can make a Living Rosary out of people literally standing or sitting in the shape of a rosary. This unique prayer service requires some advance planning, but the powerful impact it has on those who participate or witness it makes it worth it.

For this Living Rosary made out of people, each person represents one of the beads. Select a group of individuals to embody the beads of the Rosary in the church or wherever the prayer service is taking place. Each individual leads the prayer associated with his or her bead in the Rosary. You can try something beautiful like linking arms or clasping hands to join like links in a Rosary to bear witness to the power of prayer when shared together and as a way of signifying each is praying for one and all.

Raphael
"Sistine Madonna"

Bartolomé Esteban Murillo
"Virgin of the Rosary"

THE ROSARY AS MASTERPIECE

In his "Letter to Artists," Pope Saint John Paul II tells us, "Make your life a masterpiece." The Rosary is a prayerful masterpiece, a triumph of sacred beauty that shapes our lives.

The Rosary enables us to follow the advice of Philippians 4:8, To dwell upon, "whatever is true, whatever is right, whatever is pure, whatever is lovely."

And so, may we be inspired by the words of Our Lady at the Wedding at Cana when she instructs the wine stewards, "Do whatever He tells you."

Through meditating on and imitating the mysteries of the Rosary, the water of our lives can be turned into wine.

May our hands labor to make our lives a masterpiece and return again and again to the Rosary, the Sacred Braille that transforms us.

ABOUT THE AUTHOR

ANNABELLE MOSELEY is an award-winning American poet, author of nine books, Professor of Theology and host of the Catholic radio shows and podcasts on Sacramental Living: "Then Sings My Soul," and "Destination: Sainthood — Journey to the Great Cloud of Witnesses," on WCAT Radio. Moseley's work as a poet is featured as one of five artists profiled in the 2019 Documentary Film, *Masterpieces*, about the vocational call of the arts. This film is available to view through Amazon Prime and Formed On Demand (formed.org).

Moseley has won the titles of Walt Whitman Birthplace Writer-in-Residence (2009-2010) and 2014 Long Island Poet of the Year. She teaches at St. Joseph's College in New York and at St. Joseph's Seminary (Dunwoodie, NY) where she specializes in the field of Theological Aesthetics with an emphasis on the intersection between theology and literature. Moseley has led various retreats and workshops for the Diocese of Rockville Centre, New York and is the founder of Desert Bread, (desertbread.org) a series of lectures on faith and the arts that concludes with sharing a meal and taking a collection of canned food donations for local food pantries. Moseley is a frequent columnist for the Catholic online magazine, *Aleteia*.

Born on the Feast of Our Lady of the Rosary, Annabelle Moseley was baptized at the Church of St. Louis de Montfort, a saint known for his special devotion to the Rosary. Raised on the North Shore of Long Island, Moseley continues to reside there, grateful for the domestic church she has built with her husband and their children.

www.annabellemoseley.com

www.tourguideofwonder.com

To pray the Holy Rosary along with author Annabelle Moseley, featuring Sacred Braille art and poetic reflections on the Mysteries, visit **www.annabellemoseley.com/rosary/**

ALSO BY ANNABELLE MOSELEY

"Our House of the Sacred Heart: **A Litany of Stories with Art, Prayers, Poetry, and Reflections toward Consecration to the Sacred Heart"**

Whatever your story, no matter how painful, be assured that God has left signs and symbols along the way-clues to guide you to His Heart. This book, complete with beautiful prayers, devotions, art, poetry, and reflections, will teach you to spot and follow those clues, and discover your own spiritual autobiography, culminating in consecration to the Sacred Heart. Our House of the Sacred Heart is a groundbreaking collection of 33 true stories of five generations of a family formed in the Sacred Heart of Jesus through their connection to an unforgettable house. As you enter into the heart of this book, you are invited into that house and offered hospitality through time-tested stories of growth in the Faith, transiting the various gateways of life. You will be praying the Litany of the Sacred Heart while reading this work of reparation, one lesson at a time, and at book's end, consecrate yourself to the Sacred Heart of Jesus.

CPSIA information can be obtained
at www.ICGtesting.com
Printed in the USA
LVHW052000090921
697458LV00023B/3095